Spotlight On James Darren

A Journey Through Stardom, Resilience, and Timeless Influence

Sarah R. Rex

Table Of Content

Introduction

In a world where the stars of Hollywood often burn brightly but fade too soon, James Darren stands as a testament to talent, resilience, and reinvention. His journey from the bustling streets of South Philadelphia to the grand stages of Hollywood is not just a story of fame, but one of passion, determination, and the pursuit of dreams against all odds. James Darren's life is a symphony composed of diverse notes—each one playing a crucial part in the melody that has resonated with generations. As a teenager, he had a voice that made hearts race and a screen presence that captured imaginations.

But beyond the handsome face and smooth vocals lay a man driven by a love for his craft, an artist who continually sought to evolve, to explore new avenues, and to leave a lasting mark on every project he touched. This biography isn't just about the movies and songs that brought him fame. It's about the boy who dared to dream in a neighbourhood where dreams were often stifled by reality. It's about a young actor who faced rejection after rejection, yet never gave up. It's about the singer who became a teen idol, and the seasoned actor who refused to be pigeonholed into one type of role.

It's about the director who found new life behind the camera and the man who balanced stardom with the joys and challenges of family life. James Darren's story is also a reflection of a changing entertainment landscape—from the golden age of Hollywood to the dynamic world of television, and beyond. His career spans more than five decades, during which he has witnessed and adapted to the industry's many transformations. Yet through it all, his core values—integrity, humility, and an unwavering commitment to his craft—have remained constant.

As you turn these pages, you'll step into the world of a man who has lived many lives in one. You'll discover the challenges he faced, the triumphs that defined him, and the moments of doubt that tested his resolve. But most of all, you'll get to know James Darren not just as a star, but as a human being—complex, driven, and deeply passionate about his art. So, whether you've been a fan of his work for years or are just discovering his legacy, this biography will take you on a journey through the rhythm of life that is uniquely James Darren's. It's a story of perseverance, talent, and the enduring power of a dream.

Chapter 1

The Birth of a Star

In the heart of South Philadelphia, where narrow streets hum with the rhythm of daily life and families gather around their stoops, a young boy named James Darren began his journey toward stardom. His story starts not in the glitz and glamour of Hollywood, but in a modest neighbourhood where dreams often felt as distant as the stars themselves. James's early life was marked by a blend of determination and sheer will. Born James William Ercolani, he grew up in a close-knit Italian-American family where his father, a longshoreman, worked tirelessly to provide for his loved ones.

The streets of Philadelphia were his playground, and it was here, amidst the bustling markets and lively block parties, that young James first dreamed of a life beyond the confines of his hometown. From a young age, James was captivated by the world of entertainment. His passion for music and acting was nurtured in the small community theatres and local music clubs that dotted the city. The neighbourhood's local heroes, from jazz musicians to performers in tiny theatres, became his early role models.

They were the first to plant the seed of ambition in him, showing him that the world was larger than the city blocks he knew. James's family, though modest, was his greatest support. His mother, an avid fan of classic films, filled their home with music and movies. The radio played non-stop, from Frank Sinatra to Dean Martin, creating a soundtrack for his dreams. Evenings spent in front of the television watching glamorous stars made him believe that one day, he could be a part of that world. Despite the love and support from his family, the path to Hollywood was anything but smooth. James faced numerous obstacles in his quest for fame.

He was often told by critics that he didn't have the "look" or the "chops" to make it big. Rejection came frequently, but each time, it fueled his determination rather than discouraging him. He took odd jobs to support himself, from delivering groceries to working as a busboy, all while honing his craft in local clubs and auditions. In a twist of fate, James's persistence paid off when he was discovered by a talent scout while performing at a small club in Philadelphia. The scout saw something special in him, something that went beyond just his looks or his voice. It was his undeniable charisma, his passion, and his unwavering dedication. This chance encounter led to his first big break—landing a role in a television pilot that would eventually propel him into the national spotlight.

James's transition from local talent to national star was not instantaneous. He spent countless hours in auditions, often waiting in long lines with hundreds of other hopefuls. Each audition was a new challenge, and each role was a test of his talent and resolve. Yet, it was through these trials that James's true character emerged. His ability to remain hopeful and driven, despite the constant setbacks, showcased a strength that would become a hallmark of his career. During this time, the city of Philadelphia was undergoing its own transformation. The vibrant culture of the 1950s and 1960s, with its music and burgeoning arts scene, mirrored James's own journey.

The city was a melting pot of innovation and tradition, a place where new ideas clashed with old ways, creating a dynamic environment that fueled his creativity. James's rise to fame was marked by a series of pivotal moments that defined his early career. His breakthrough came with a role in a popular TV show that showcased his talent to a broader audience. The role was a departure from his earlier work, presenting him as a charming and versatile actor. This part allowed him to break free from the typecasting that had previously limited his opportunities. As his popularity grew, so did the attention from the media.

James was suddenly in the limelight, with paparazzi snapping photos and journalists eager to interview him. Despite the whirlwind of fame, he remained grounded, never forgetting his roots in South Philadelphia. He often spoke about the influence of his upbringing and the values instilled in him by his family. His humility and gratitude were as much a part of his public persona as his talent. Today, James Darren's story serves as an inspiring example of perseverance and dedication. From his humble beginnings in Philadelphia to his rise as a star, his journey is a testament to the power of dreams and the importance of staying true to oneself.

As we look back on the early days of his career, it's clear that the boy from South Philadelphia was destined for greatness. His story is not just about achieving fame but about the relentless pursuit of a dream and the unwavering belief in oneself. This chapter captures the essence of James Darren's beginnings—his struggles, his victories, and the early signs of the star he was to become. It's a reminder that even the brightest stars start from the simplest of places, and that with passion and determination, dreams can become reality.

Chapter 2

Breaking into Hollywood; The Struggles, Sacrifices, and Sweet Success

In the heart of the 1950s, Hollywood was a land of dreams and dilemmas, a place where the pursuit of stardom was as fraught with challenges as it was filled with glittering promises. For James Darren, breaking into this glamorous but gruelling world was an arduous journey marked by relentless struggle and small victories. James Darren arrived in Hollywood with a heart full of ambition and a suitcase full of hope. He was not alone in this quest; the city was crowded with aspiring actors, each one vying for their chance in the spotlight.

The early days for James were not filled with instant fame but rather with the harsh realities of auditions and rejections. He faced numerous setbacks, each one a test of his resolve and determination. One of the most trying aspects of breaking into Hollywood was the constant rejection. James found himself in long lines at casting calls, competing against countless others for the same roles. Each audition was a chance to prove himself, but also a potential setback when he didn't land the part.

Despite these challenges, James never lost faith in his dream. His resilience was his greatest asset. He learned to accept rejection with grace and use it as fuel to drive his next performance. A turning point in James Darren's journey came when he landed a small role in a television show. It was a modest start, but it gave him the exposure he needed. The role, though minor, was his first taste of what it was like to be part of a production. It introduced him to the world of television and provided a stepping stone to bigger opportunities. This early role was a testament to his perseverance and an indication of the talent that would soon captivate audiences nationwide.

At the same time, Hollywood was changing. The film industry was evolving, and the demand for fresh faces and new talent was growing. This period saw the rise of the "teen idol" phenomenon, and James Darren was well-positioned to take advantage of this trend. The young actors who captured the hearts of teenage audiences were becoming stars in their own right, and James was about to make his mark in this new wave of stardom. The defining moment in James Darren's career came with his role in the film "Gidget." It was a role that would set the stage for his future successes. Playing the charming Moondoggie, James quickly became a teen heartthrob. The film's success was a testament to his ability to connect with audiences and his skill in bringing characters to life.

The film was a hit, and James's performance was widely praised. His charm, good looks, and natural acting ability made him a standout in a crowded field. The success of "Gidget" opened doors for James. He began to receive more offers and his career started to gain momentum. However, the path to success was still filled with challenges. The pressure to maintain his newfound fame was immense. James had to navigate the pitfalls of celebrity while continuing to hone his craft. It was a delicate balance between staying relevant and avoiding the trappings of fame that had ensnared many before him.

In parallel with his rise to fame, Hollywood itself was undergoing significant changes. The film industry was experiencing a shift, with new trends and technologies shaping the way movies were made and consumed. James Darren adapted to these changes, embracing new opportunities and expanding his range as an actor. His versatility became one of his greatest strengths, allowing him to take on a variety of roles and maintain his relevance in a rapidly evolving industry. The success of James Darren's early career was not just about talent; it was also about timing and tenacity. He arrived in Hollywood at a moment when the industry was ready for fresh faces and new stories. His ability to seize this opportunity and make the most of it was a testament to his dedication and hard work.

As James Darren's career continued to flourish, he remained grounded. Despite the whirlwind of fame, he never forgot the struggles he faced or the lessons he learned along the way. He continued to work tirelessly, always striving to improve and to take on new challenges. His journey from a struggling actor to a beloved star was a testament to his resilience and his passion for his craft.

This chapter of James Darren's biography highlights the trials and triumphs of breaking into Hollywood. It is a story of perseverance, sacrifice, and eventual success. Through his struggles and his victories, James Darren emerged as a star who captured the hearts of audiences and left a lasting impact on the entertainment industry. His journey serves as an inspiring reminder of the power of determination and the importance of never giving up on one's dreams.

Chapter 3

A Voice That Captivates – The Music That Made Him a Teen Idol

In the early 1960s, while Hollywood was buzzing with the latest film stars, James Darren was carving out his place in a different realm of entertainment. He had already made a name for himself as an actor, but a new chapter was about to unfold—one that would elevate him to the heights of teen idol fame. This chapter of his life was all about music, and it was here that James Darren truly began to captivate the hearts of millions. James's foray into music wasn't just a career move; it was a passion that had been brewing since his teenage years in Philadelphia.

The city had been a fertile ground for his musical ambitions, filled with vibrant clubs and talented musicians. By the time he was ready to step into the recording studio, James was not only prepared but eager to make a splash in the world of music. The magic began with the release of his debut single, "Bewitched, Bothered and Bewildered." It wasn't just a song—it was a declaration of James Darren's arrival as a serious music artist.

The track was a blend of classic charm and modern appeal, featuring his smooth vocals and a catchy melody that resonated with a wide audience. The single quickly climbed the charts, marking the beginning of his music career with great success. The success of "Bewitched, Bothered and Bewildered" opened doors to more opportunities. James Darren soon found himself in recording studios, working with top-notch producers and talented musicians. The experience of recording became a thrilling part of his life, filled with late-night sessions, creative brainstorming, and the excitement of hearing his voice on the radio for the first time.

One of the most significant moments in James's musical career came with the release of his hit song "Goodbye Cruel World." The track was a perfect example of his ability to capture the zeitgeist of the era, blending a heartfelt melody with lyrics that spoke to the feelings of young listeners. The song became an anthem for many, reflecting the emotions of a generation caught between innocence and the complexities of growing up. Its success further cemented James's place as a leading teen idol and showcased his talent as a singer. During this time, James Darren's popularity soared. He was featured on television shows, performing live and charming audiences with his charisma.

His appearances on shows like "The Ed Sullivan Show" and "American Bandstand" were memorable, filled with energy and excitement. Each performance was a chance for James to connect with his fans and share his music with the world. Despite the whirlwind of fame, James remained grounded. He often spoke about the importance of staying true to oneself and not letting fame overshadow the passion for the craft. His dedication to music was evident in every performance, every recording, and every interaction with his fans. He continued to work hard, always striving to improve and to create music that resonated with his audience.

The influence of James Darren's music extended beyond the United States. As he toured internationally, his songs found new audiences and new fans. The global reach of his music was a testament to its universal appeal and his ability to connect with people from different cultures. His tours were met with enthusiasm and adoration, and he embraced the opportunity to perform for audiences around the world. James's success in music was not just about his voice or his songs; it was also about the way he connected with his fans. His charm, his sincerity, and his genuine love for performing made him a beloved figure. He was not just a teen idol; he was a symbol of the era, a reflection of the dreams and aspirations of young people everywhere.

As the 1960s came to a close, James Darren's career in music continued to thrive. He released several more albums and singles, each one adding to his legacy as a talented and versatile artist. His contributions to music were recognized with awards and accolades, and he remained a prominent figure in the industry. Today, James Darren's musical legacy is celebrated as an integral part of his career. His songs continue to be enjoyed by new generations, and his influence on the world of music is undeniable.

The chapter of his life that saw him rise as a teen idol was a crucial part of his journey, showcasing his talent, his dedication, and his ability to capture the essence of an era. This chapter highlights the exciting and transformative period of his musical career. It's a story of passion, success, and the ability to connect with audiences through the power of song. James Darren's voice not only captivated the hearts of millions but also left an indelible mark on the world of music, proving that his talent was as boundless as his dreams.

Chapter 4

Reinventing a Star

James Darren's career was far from a single, predictable path. By the late 1960s, he stood at a crossroads that would define his future: the choice to stick with what he knew or to boldly venture into new territories. As Hollywood and the world around him evolved, so did James, demonstrating a remarkable ability to reinvent himself and adapt to changing times. The turning point came with a remarkable shift in James's career. He was no longer just a teen idol with a pretty face and a smooth voice. The landscape of entertainment was evolving, and so was James. The early 70s saw him embracing roles that were more complex and dramatic.

This transition wasn't just a career move; it was a testament to his versatility and willingness to explore different facets of his talent. James's decision to pivot from his established persona came with its own set of challenges. The shift from being a teen heartthrob to a serious actor required him to prove his range and depth. He took on roles that were far from the charming characters he had previously portrayed. One of his most notable performances during this time was in the television drama "The FBI," where he played a gritty, morally ambiguous character.

This role was a significant departure from his previous work, showcasing his ability to handle complex, nuanced characters. Despite his success in these new roles, the transition was not without its hurdles. The industry was often resistant to change, and James faced scepticism from critics and peers alike. There were whispers that his new direction was a gamble, and some wondered if he could truly reinvent himself. However, James's determination and hard work spoke volumes. He threw himself into every role with passion, earning respect and proving that he was more than just a passing trend.

The 1970s also marked a period of personal growth and change for James Darren. He became more involved in behind-the-scenes work, exploring opportunities as a director and producer. This move allowed him to shape projects from the ground up and to bring his creative vision to life. His work behind the camera was a natural extension of his acting career, showcasing his deep understanding of the industry and his commitment to storytelling. During this period, James also took time to reflect on his career and his impact on the industry. He recognized the importance of evolving with the times and embracing new opportunities. This self-awareness was crucial in helping him stay relevant and successful in a rapidly changing entertainment landscape.

He also remained dedicated to his fans, often sharing his journey and his new projects with them, maintaining a close connection with his audience. One of the most significant projects of this era was his involvement in the television series "T.J. Hooker." The show, which began in the early 1980s, was a departure from the roles James had previously played. It featured him as a tough, street-smart cop, a role that was both challenging and rewarding. The series became a hit, and James's performance was widely praised. His ability to embrace such a different character was a testament to his acting range and his willingness to take risks.

The success of "T.J. Hooker" solidified James Darren's place as a versatile actor capable of taking on a wide range of roles. It also demonstrated his enduring appeal and his ability to adapt to new trends and formats. The series was a hit with audiences and critics alike, and it marked a new chapter in James's career, showcasing his talent in a different light. James's journey through this period of reinvention was not just about changing his roles; it was also about embracing new opportunities and exploring different aspects of his career. His work as a director and producer allowed him to expand his influence in the industry and to contribute to projects in new and meaningful ways.

His ability to adapt and evolve kept him at the forefront of the entertainment world, proving that he was not just a star of the past but a dynamic and evolving talent. As James Darren moved into the late 1980s and beyond, his career continued to flourish. He embraced new roles and opportunities, demonstrating that his talent and versatility were as strong as ever. His journey was a testament to his ability to reinvent himself and to stay relevant in an ever-changing industry.

This chapter captures the essence of his career transformation. It's a story of reinvention, resilience, and the pursuit of new challenges. James Darren's ability to adapt and evolve, while staying true to his passion for entertainment, is a testament to his enduring talent and his unwavering commitment to his craft. His journey through this period of change and growth serves as an inspiring example of what it means to be a true artist.

Chapter 5

Embracing Challenges and New Horizons

In the mid-1980s, as James Darren stood at a crossroads in his career, he faced a choice that would redefine his path. The glitter of Hollywood was familiar, but the desire to explore new horizons and embrace different challenges was stronger than ever. This chapter of his life was marked by a series of bold decisions and unexpected opportunities that showcased his adventurous spirit and resilience. The turning point began with a surprising twist: James Darren's decision to take on roles outside his usual comfort zone. It was not just a career move but a statement of his willingness to embrace the unknown.

The world of entertainment was evolving, and James was determined to keep pace by stepping into new and diverse roles that pushed his boundaries. One of the most striking examples of this adventurous phase was his foray into theatre. James took a leap into the world of live performance, a realm that was both exhilarating and daunting. His stage debut was met with curiosity and anticipation. The transition from the screen to the stage was no small feat, but James embraced the challenge with enthusiasm and dedication.

The play, a dramatic piece with deep emotional undertones, allowed James to showcase his acting skills in a new light. The experience was intense and demanding, but it also proved to be incredibly rewarding. His performance received acclaim from critics and audiences alike, further proving his versatility and commitment to his craft. The stage became a new canvas for James, one where he could explore different facets of his talent and connect with audiences in a more immediate and intimate way. During this period, James Darren also embarked on an international tour, performing in countries around the world. The tour was a significant undertaking, involving numerous performances and travel across various continents.

It was a chance for James to reach new audiences and to experience different cultures. The tour was a mix of exhilarating and exhausting moments, but it was a testament to his dedication and passion for his work. The international tour brought with it a unique set of challenges and rewards. Performing in different countries exposed James to new perspectives and artistic traditions. Each city had its own character, and each performance was a unique experience. The tour allowed him to build connections with fans from diverse backgrounds and to share his love for music and acting with a global audience.

Back in the United States, James continued to explore new opportunities. He ventured into producing, using his experience and insights to shape new projects. His work behind the scenes was a natural extension of his career, allowing him to contribute to the industry in meaningful ways. The projects he produced were varied, reflecting his wide-ranging interests and his desire to bring innovative stories to life. One of the most exciting developments during this time was James's involvement in a groundbreaking television series. The show, which combined elements of drama and science fiction, was a departure from traditional formats. It challenged conventional storytelling and provided James with a platform to experiment with new ideas.

His role in the series was complex and multifaceted, offering him a chance to showcase his range and adaptability. The series quickly gained a following, and James's performance was widely praised. The show became a cultural touchstone, reflecting the evolving tastes and interests of viewers. James's involvement in such a forward-thinking project was a testament to his willingness to embrace change and to push the boundaries of his career. Throughout this period, James Darren's career was characterised by a sense of adventure and a willingness to take risks. He embraced new challenges with enthusiasm and demonstrated a remarkable ability to adapt to changing times.

His journey was a series of bold steps and creative endeavours, each one contributing to his legacy as a versatile and dynamic performer. As James moved into the 1990s, he continued to build on the successes of this transformative period. His career was a reflection of his passion for his craft and his commitment to exploring new possibilities. The road less travelled had been filled with challenges, but it also offered rich rewards and opportunities for growth.

Chapter Five of James Darren's biography is a celebration of his willingness to embrace change and pursue new horizons. It is a story of adventure, resilience, and the courage to take risks. James Darren's journey during this time highlights his dedication to his craft and his ability to reinvent himself, proving that true artistry is not just about staying relevant but about continuously evolving and exploring new paths. His experiences during this period are a testament to his enduring talent and his unyielding spirit.

Chapter 6

A New Chapter – The Renaissance of James Darren

As the 1990s unfolded, James Darren found himself at a crossroads of a different kind. The world around him was shifting, and so was his place within it. After decades of navigating the entertainment industry, James faced an opportunity to reinvent himself once again, diving into new projects and embracing fresh challenges that would redefine his legacy.

The dawn of this new era began with an unexpected but exciting venture into the world of reality television. This genre, then emerging as a powerful force in media, offered James a unique platform to connect with audiences in a different way. He joined a popular reality show that combined elements of celebrity competition with behind-the-scenes insights into the lives of its participants. For James, it was more than just a new project; it was an opportunity to show a more personal side of himself and to engage with fans in a way he hadn't before.

The reality show was a rollercoaster of experiences. James navigated the challenges with his characteristic charm and resilience, gaining admiration not only for his skills but also for his authenticity. His participation in the show was met with widespread enthusiasm, and viewers were captivated by the blend of celebrity allure and real-life drama. This experience was not only a testament to James's adaptability but also a reminder of his enduring appeal across different formats and genres. During this period, James also turned his attention to charitable causes. He became actively involved in various philanthropic efforts, using his influence to support causes close to his heart.

From fundraising events to public awareness campaigns, James worked tirelessly to make a difference. His involvement in charity was a new facet of his public persona, showcasing his commitment to giving back and highlighting his deep sense of responsibility beyond the spotlight. One notable project was his support for children's education initiatives. James participated in a high-profile charity event aimed at raising funds for underprivileged schools. The event was a success, drawing attention to the importance of education and highlighting the needs of underserved communities. James's dedication to the cause resonated with many, reinforcing his reputation as not only a talented entertainer but also a compassionate individual.

As the millennium approached, James Darren's career took another intriguing turn with his return to music. This time, he was not just revisiting old hits but exploring new musical landscapes. He released an album that blended classic sounds with contemporary influences, reflecting his ability to bridge the gap between past and present. The album was a celebration of his journey through music, offering a fresh take on his well-loved style while introducing new elements that resonated with modern audiences. The release of this album was met with critical acclaim and commercial success. The songs featured on the album were a mix of original tracks and reimagined classics, each one showcasing James's versatility and enduring talent.

The project was a reminder of his ability to evolve and adapt, demonstrating that even after decades in the industry, he remained a vibrant and influential force in music. In addition to his musical endeavours, James also took on new acting roles that further demonstrated his range. He appeared in several acclaimed television series and films, each role adding depth to his already impressive career. His performances were characterised by a renewed energy and passion, reflecting his ongoing commitment to his craft. One of the standout projects of this period was his role in a critically acclaimed miniseries.

The series was a dramatic portrayal of historical events, and James's performance was widely praised for its depth and authenticity. The role allowed him to explore complex characters and narratives, further solidifying his status as a versatile and respected actor. As the 2000s began, James Darren's career was a tapestry of diverse achievements. He had successfully navigated the evolving entertainment landscape, embracing new opportunities and challenges with grace and determination.

His journey through this period was a testament to his resilience and his ability to continually reinvent himself. This chapter captures a time of transformation and renewal. It is a story of adaptation and growth, highlighting James's ability to embrace new formats, explore charitable endeavours, and continue his artistic journey with vigour and passion. His experiences during this era reflect a deep commitment to his craft and a profound connection with his audience, proving that even after years in the industry, James Darren remained a dynamic and influential figure.

Chapter 7

Family and Fame; Balancing a Life in the Spotlight

James Darren's life was a delicate dance between the glitz of Hollywood and the warmth of family. Born James William Ercolani on June 8, 1936, Darren emerged as one of the most celebrated figures of his time. His transformation from a teen idol to a respected actor, singer, and director was closely intertwined with his efforts to maintain a balanced personal life amidst the pressures of fame.

James's journey into the limelight began with his role as Moondoggie in the beloved film Gidget (1959). The movie, a quintessential representation of the surfing craze of the 1950s, catapulted him to fame and made him a household name. His charm and talent resonated with audiences, and soon, his musical career took off with hits like "Goodbye Cruel World" and "Her Royal Majesty," both of which climbed the Billboard Hot 100 charts. Despite this whirlwind of success, James never lost sight of what mattered most: his family. James's personal life saw its share of highs and lows.

His first marriage was to Gloria, with whom he had a son, Jim Moret. Jim would go on to become a prominent journalist, reflecting James's influence in both his professional and personal spheres. However, the marriage eventually ended in divorce, marking a significant shift in James's life. Following this change, James found new love with Evy Norlund, a former Miss Universe contestant. Their marriage brought new joy and a sense of stability, and together they had two sons, Christian and Anthony. Evy's presence in James's life was a grounding force, helping him navigate the complexities of his career while raising a family.

Their partnership was a testament to James's ability to find balance amidst the chaos of fame. One of the most intriguing aspects of James's life was his role as a godfather to Nancy Sinatra's daughter, A.J. Lambert. This connection to another iconic family added an extra layer of depth to James's personal and professional relationships. The bond with Nancy Sinatra and her family was a testament to the close-knit community of stars and their intertwining lives. It also highlighted James's role as a supportive and caring friend, beyond the glitz of his own career. Despite the demands of his profession, James was committed to balancing his family life with his public persona. He understood the pressures of fame and took deliberate steps to ensure his family remained his top priority.

His efforts to manage his personal and professional responsibilities were reflected in his approach to his career, including his work as a director on popular television series like Beverly Hills, 90210 and Melrose Place. These projects were not just career milestones but also ways for him to provide stability and financial security for his family. James's dedication to his family was evident in the way he spoke about them in interviews and public appearances. He often mentioned how much he valued their support and how they provided him with a sense of normalcy. His family was not just a part of his life; they were the foundation that kept him grounded amidst the whirlwind of fame.

The balancing act between personal life and public attention was not without its challenges. James faced the scrutiny of the media and the expectations of being a public figure while striving to be a present and supportive father and husband. The pressures of fame were ever-present, but his commitment to his family was unwavering. He made a concerted effort to ensure that his personal relationships remained strong, despite the demands of his career. James Darren's legacy is not only defined by his contributions to entertainment but also by his ability to navigate the complexities of fame while maintaining a strong and supportive family life.

His journey was marked by a series of successful projects and personal milestones, each reflecting his dedication to both his craft and his loved ones. As the years passed, James continued to balance his roles as a performer and family man with grace and resilience. His story is a reminder that behind the public persona of a celebrated star lies a person who values family, stability, and personal connections.

Chapter Seven of James Darren's biography delves into the intricate dance of balancing fame with family. It is a story of dedication, love, and the pursuit of happiness amidst the demands of a high-profile career. James Darren's life, both on and off the screen, is a testament to his ability to harmonise his personal and professional worlds, proving that true success is measured not just in accolades but in the love and support of those closest to us.

Chapter 8

Facing the Music – Overcoming Obstacles and Reinventing His Career

James Darren's journey through the entertainment world reads like a story of triumph over adversity. Born James William Ercolani on June 8, 1936, in Philadelphia, Darren's early rise to fame was nothing short of meteoric. However, the road to success was not always smooth. It was a path marked by reinvention, resilience, and the unyielding spirit of an artist who continually faced the music, both literally and metaphorically.

In the late 1950s, James Darren was catapulted into the spotlight with his role as Moondoggie in *Gidget* (1959). The film captured the spirit of the surfing craze and made Darren a teenage heartthrob. His subsequent musical hits, such as "Goodbye Cruel World," solidified his status as a pop sensation. But fame, as Darren quickly discovered, came with its own set of challenges. The studio system, which initially promised glamour and success, soon began to confine him. "I felt like a prisoner," Darren later admitted, reflecting on the limitations imposed by his early career.

The pressure to maintain his teen idol status led to repetitive roles and sequels, such as Gidget Goes Hawaiian(1961) and Gidget Goes to Rome (1963), which left him longing for more creative freedom. As the 1960s wound down, Darren faced the inevitable decline of his film career. Instead of succumbing to despair, he shifted gears and embraced the world of television. The transition was far from a retreat; it was a strategic move that allowed him to explore new roles and stay relevant in the industry. Darren made notable appearances on popular shows like *The Time Tunnel*, *Hawaii Five-O*, and *The Love Boat*. Each role was a step toward redefining his career and showcasing his versatility.

The 1980s marked a significant turning point. James Darren took a bold step behind the camera, embracing a new role as a director. He directed episodes for notable television series such as *Beverly Hills, 90210* and *Melrose Place*. This transition was not just a career pivot but a testament to his adaptability and willingness to embrace change. Darren's directorial work allowed him to influence the entertainment world in new ways, shaping narratives rather than just performing them. It was a role that extended his career and cemented his influence in Hollywood.

In the 1990s, Darren faced a new set of challenges and opportunities. This decade saw a resurgence in his popularity, particularly through his role as Vic Fontaine on *Star Trek: Deep Space Nine*. Portraying a holographic lounge singer, Darren connected with a new generation of fans. His performance was more than a nod to nostalgia; it was a reinvention that showcased his enduring talent. The character of Vic Fontaine allowed Darren to blend his musical talents with his acting skills, creating a memorable and beloved role that resonated with viewers.

The resilience James Darren displayed throughout his career is a testament to his spirit and determination. He once remarked, "Every career has its hills and valleys... The most important thing is that you are happy with yourself." This perspective highlights Darren's understanding that success is not a straight path but a journey with ups and downs. His ability to continually seek new opportunities and adapt to changing circumstances was a key factor in his enduring success. In his later years, James Darren's career continued to reflect his diverse talents and interests. His contributions to film, music, and television were marked by an unwavering commitment to his craft. Even as he faced the challenges of aging and the evolving entertainment industry, Darren remained active and engaged.

His final years were a celebration of his legacy, showcasing the depth and breadth of his contributions to the world of entertainment. James Darren's passing on September 2, 2024, marked the end of an era for many who had grown up watching his films or listening to his music. His legacy is one of resilience and reinvention, a reminder that true success lies in the ability to face obstacles with grace and emerge stronger. Darren's journey through the highs and lows of his career serves as an inspiring story of an artist who faced the music and came out with a legacy that continues to inspire and captivate.

Chapter 9

The Legacy Lives On – Influence on Generations of Entertainers

James Darren's name resonates with an undeniable charm that transcends generations. Born James William Ercolani on June 8, 1936, Darren's journey from a teenage heartthrob to a revered actor and director is a story of resilience and lasting influence. Even after his passing on September 2, 2024, at the age of 88, Darren's legacy remains a beacon for aspiring entertainers and a symbol of enduring appeal.

James Darren's career was a remarkable journey through multiple facets of the entertainment industry. He first captured the public's imagination with his role as Moondoggie in the film Gidget (1959). This role catapulted him to fame as a teen idol, and his charisma was undeniable. Darren's performance in Gidget not only showcased his acting chops but also highlighted his musical talent. His subsequent reprisal of Moondoggie in Gidget Goes Hawaiian (1961) and Gidget Goes to Rome (1963) solidified his status as a pop culture icon.

Darren's success extended beyond the realm of teen idols. He ventured into a diverse array of roles, including his memorable appearances in *The Guns of Navarone* (1961) and *Diamond Head* (1962). His musical career flourished as well, with hits like "Goodbye Cruel World" making a significant impact on the Billboard Hot 100. These achievements marked Darren as a versatile entertainer who could captivate audiences across various mediums. The 1960s brought inevitable changes to Darren's career as the film industry shifted and his teen idol status began to wane.

Rather than fading from the limelight, Darren reinvented himself by transitioning to television. His roles in the sci-fi series; The Time Tunnel and guest appearances on shows like Hawaii Five-O and The Love Boat showcased his ability to adapt and remain relevant in the ever-changing entertainment landscape. The 1980s were a pivotal period for Darren, marking his shift from actor to director. He took on the challenge of directing episodes for popular television series, including *Beverly Hills, 90210* and *Melrose Place*. This new role allowed Darren to influence the industry from behind the scenes, demonstrating his versatility and willingness to embrace change. His directorial work not only extended his career but also highlighted his talent for guiding and shaping narratives.Despite the evolving entertainment landscape, James Darren's popularity endured. The 1990s saw a resurgence in his fame through his role as Vic Fontaine on *Star Trek: Deep Space Nine*. This character, a holographic lounge singer, resonated with both old fans and a new generation. Darren's portrayal of Vic Fontaine brought a sense of nostalgia while also showcasing his continued talent as a singer and actor. The role was a testament to his ability to connect with audiences across different eras. Darren's iconic roles, such as Moondoggie and Vic Fontaine, have left a lasting imprint on popular culture. Moondoggie represents the quintessential surfer boy of the 1950s, while Vic Fontaine embodies the suave, charming entertainer of the 1990s.

These characters have become embedded in the collective memory of audiences, illustrating Darren's ability to create memorable and beloved roles. James Darren's personal life was as remarkable as his professional career. His two marriages, first to Gloria Terlitsky and later to Evy Norlund, resulted in three children who have followed in his footsteps. His son, James Darren Jr., has pursued a career in entertainment, while his other sons, Christian and Anthony, have also been influenced by their father's legacy. Darren's commitment to his family was evident in the way he balanced his career with his responsibilities as a husband and father.

His children's pursuit of careers in the entertainment industry reflects the lasting influence of Darren's values and work ethic. His dedication to his family, combined with his professional achievements, paints a picture of a man who successfully navigated the complexities of fame while remaining grounded. James Darren's passing on September 2, 2024, marked the end of an era for many who had grown up watching him on screen or listening to his music. However, his legacy continues to thrive through the countless performers he has inspired and the indelible mark he has left on the entertainment industry. Tributes from fellow actors and fans alike underscore the profound impact Darren had on those who knew him. William Shatner's heartfelt message on social media, describing Darren as "a wonderful man – so talented; so loving," captures the sentiment shared by many who had the privilege of working with him. Darren's legacy is not just about his roles and hits but also about the inspiration he provided to countless entertainers. James Darren's life and career stand as a testament to the power of talent, adaptability, and enduring appeal. From his early days as a teen idol to his later successes as a director and beloved character actor, Darren's journey exemplifies the essence of a true entertainer. As the world continues to celebrate his contributions, James Darren's memory will live on through his timeless performances and the generations of performers he has inspired.

Chapter 10

Legacy and Reflection

James Darren's story is not merely one of success in the entertainment world; it is a chronicle of resilience, transformation, and profound influence. As he approached the twilight of his life, Darren reflected on a career that had spanned over six decades, leaving an indelible mark on the worlds of film, music, and television. This chapter explores how Darren's legacy continues to resonate, his reflections on a lifetime in the spotlight, and the impact he made as he looked back on his remarkable journey.

By the early 2020s, James Darren had achieved a rare status in the entertainment industry. His name was not only a reminder of classic films and hit songs but also a symbol of adaptability and enduring talent. Darren's final public appearances were a testament to his ongoing influence. Whether he was reminiscing about his iconic roles or discussing the evolution of the industry, his insights were eagerly sought after. His reflections were often marked by a deep sense of nostalgia but also a forward-looking perspective that inspired many.

In 2022, Darren participated in a high-profile interview for a documentary series celebrating classic Hollywood legends. During this interview, he spoke candidly about his experiences with fame, the challenges of transitioning from a teen idol to a respected actor and director, and the changing dynamics of the entertainment industry. His comments about how the industry had evolved, especially with the rise of digital media and streaming platforms, offered a glimpse into the mind of an artist who had navigated numerous shifts in the industry.

James Darren's reflections were often laced with gratitude for the opportunities he had been given and the people he had worked with. He frequently spoke about the importance of reinvention and the lessons he learned from his early struggles. Darren acknowledged that while the fame of his youth had its challenges, it also provided him with a platform to evolve and influence new generations. One poignant moment in his final years came when he attended a charity event honouring his contributions to entertainment. The event, held in Los Angeles in 2023, brought together many of his former colleagues and fans. It was here that Darren, surrounded by friends and family, took the stage to deliver a heartfelt speech. He spoke about the joy of seeing young artists who had been inspired by his work and the satisfaction of knowing that his influence had extended beyond his own era. His speech was a moving reminder of how one's legacy can transcend time and continue to impact others. In the years leading up to his passing, Darren was involved in several projects that highlighted his enduring influence. He collaborated with emerging artists and directors, providing mentorship and guidance. His involvement in these projects was not just about sharing his experience but also about fostering new talent and helping them navigate their own journeys in the entertainment industry.

One notable project was a musical tribute album released in 2023, featuring contemporary artists covering some of Darren's classic hits. The album received widespread acclaim and introduced Darren's music to a new generation of listeners. The success of this project demonstrated how Darren's artistry continued to resonate, even as the music landscape evolved. Additionally, Darren's influence was evident in various film and television retrospectives that celebrated his career. Documentaries and special programs aired on major networks, exploring his contributions to the industry and the impact of his work. These retrospectives often included interviews with fellow actors, directors, and musicians who shared their experiences working with Darren and how he had influenced their own careers.

James Darren passed away on September 2, 2024, leaving behind a legacy that continues to inspire. His funeral, attended by a multitude of fans, friends, and colleagues, was a celebration of his life and career. It was a moment of reflection for many who had been touched by his work and a testament to the lasting impact of his contributions. As the world mourned his passing, tributes poured in from across the entertainment industry. Many spoke of Darren's generosity, his dedication to his craft, and his role as a mentor and inspiration to others. His legacy was not just about his on-screen achievements but also about the way he had lived his life—with grace, resilience, and a commitment to leaving a positive mark on the world.

James Darren's life and career offer a powerful narrative of influence and transformation. His ability to adapt, reinvent himself, and inspire others is a testament to his enduring legacy. As the entertainment world continues to evolve, Darren's contributions remain a guiding light for future generations of performers. His story is a reminder that true legacy is not just about the accolades one receives but about the impact one has on others and the world. James Darren's journey through time is a remarkable tale of talent, perseverance, and lasting influence, ensuring that his legacy will continue to shine brightly for years to come.

Conclusion

James Darren's life was a masterclass in perseverance, adaptability, and enduring charm. From his rise as a teenage heartthrob to his evolution into a versatile actor, singer, and director, Darren's journey through the entertainment industry exemplifies the power of resilience and transformation. His career spanned over six decades, marked by a remarkable ability to reinvent himself and continue influencing new generations of performers. The narrative of Darren's life is not just about the roles he played or the hits he recorded. It's about the indelible mark he left on the entertainment world and the people who knew him.

His iconic portrayal of Moondoggie in *Gidget* and his later success as Vic Fontaine in *Star Trek: Deep Space Nine* are just highlights of a career that demonstrated his broad range and adaptability. But beyond the accolades and achievements, Darren's true legacy lies in his ability to connect with audiences and his unwavering commitment to his craft. In his final years, James Darren reflected on his remarkable journey with humility and grace. He understood that the essence of his legacy was not just in the nostalgic memories of his past roles but in the inspiration he provided to others.

His influence extended beyond the silver screen and recording studio, touching the lives of countless individuals who admired his work and learned from his example. The outpouring of tributes and heartfelt messages following his passing on September 2, 2024, underscored the profound impact Darren had on those who knew him and the world at large. From his peers in the entertainment industry to the fans who grew up with his music and movies, James Darren's legacy is celebrated as a beacon of talent and resilience.

As we reflect on the life of James Darren, we remember not just the achievements of a beloved entertainer but the spirit of an artist who faced challenges head-on and emerged with a legacy that continues to inspire. His story is a testament to the power of creativity, the importance of adaptability, and the enduring nature of true talent. James Darren's life serves as a reminder that a meaningful legacy is built not just on success but on the impact one leaves on others and the joy one brings to the world. In celebrating James Darren, we honour a life well-lived and a career that, through its many phases, always remains a testament to the enduring power of art and the human spirit. His story will continue to inspire, entertain, and remind us all of the beauty of a life dedicated to passion and perseverance.